NutriBullet Blender Cookbook for Beginners

Foolproof Recipes to Lose Weight, Gain Energy, and Feel Great

Brance Daren

information contained within this document, including, but not limited to, errors, omissions, or inaccuracies.

Table of contents

Introduction

The smoothie industry has seen a boom in the recent decade, and more people are turning to this lifestyle. Fruits and vegetables have always been good for us, and dieticians recommend having at least 2 ½ cups of different vegetables and 2 cups of a variety of fresh fruits every day. The fresh produce plays a vital role in reducing risks of cancer, heart diseases, and stroke, and the best of all, managing the weight. A cup of blended fruits and vegetables like smoothies can reap serious benefits for you as it holds the reputation as a health food. If you are interested in drinking up your food rather than eating it, then this e-book is for you. I have been in your place where I was charmed by the easy and simple life, I could lead by blending my foods, and it sure worked for me. But there was a huge obstacle staring in my face – a convenient blender for this job. Indeed, it is exhausting to find the best blender that not comes with multiple features but has to be budget-friendly as well. My search and experiments finally led me to "Nutribullet Blender ZNBF30400Z Machine," which ticks all the boxes of my requirements.

If you are looking for a budget blender, then you cannot go wrong with the NutriBullet Blender ZNBF30400Z Machine.

Chapter 1: NutriBullet–More Than A Blender

Benefits of NutriBullet Blender

Nutribullet Blender ZNBF30400Z is not just a blender; it is so much more.

- High-powered Nutribullet Blender ZNBF30400Z does a perfect job of blending any recipe precisely and quickly.
- It is even more excellent at grinding hard ingredients and pureeing sauces and condiments, whipping up soups, and beyond, which other blenders cannot.
- Life gets more comfortable with its simple controls for pulsing function and multiple speed blends.
- It gives you full control of the blending process at the press of a button.
- Although this blender lacks a digital timer and automatic preset blending function, so you have to control the duration of blending manually, but it's not too much work.

Blending Vs Juicing

There has always been a debate between which one is the best – blending or juicing?

With juicing, ingredients lose their all fibrous materials and leave only liquid of product. However, with blending, you get everything, the fiber and fiber, with which the produce is loaded. Both juicing and blending come with their benefits.

Juicing:

- The juice is more concentrated with nutrients and vitamins.
- The nutrients are easier to absorb.
- Most of the juices contain a high amount of sugar, even greater than sodas.

- Juices lack fiber, which is essential for proper digestion, lowers the risk of heart diseases, maintain the blood sugar level, and improves health.

Blending:

- Blending retain all the nutrients, vitamins and fibers of vegetables and fruits which is essential for healthy digestions
- It is also rich in antioxidants.
- The fiber in blended food makes you fill-up.

To sum up, juicing your food has a variety of benefits. It increases the consumption of vegetables and fruits, has a greater concentration of nutrients, and enhance the absorption of nutrients. Juicing is great for individuals who face difficulty to stomach the taste of their vegetables and fruits. On the other hand, you are also missing out on important fiber and other compounds that are present in the peel and pulp of the produce.

On the other hand, with blending, you get the produce has to offer. Moreover, we are basically cutting out one step by mechanically breaking down of food, and this saves your stomach from doing the hard work of breaking food down itself. Some vegetables like cauliflower are hard to digest and often lead to upset stomach, inflammation, or bloating. So, blending the hard ingredients is an amazing way to maintain the health of your gut. Plus, this is particularly beneficial for the people on-the-go who are not really interested in chewing their food.

Why You Should Buy a NutriBullet?

Investing your hard-earned money for buying the NutriBullet blender is a smart decision and really worth it. Here are the following reasons:

1. Break down ingredients to the molecular level

Most of the blender in the market does a good job of blending ingredients, but they don't exactly breakdown the food thoroughly. Nutribullet is specifically designed to break down the hardest and even the smallest ingredients, and this turns the smoothest smoothies. Nutribullet blender helps in unlocking fatty acids (omega-3), minerals, and vitamins that have trapped in the peel of the fruits, veggies, seeds, and nuts. Moreover, its laser-cut blender and high-powered motor are enough to turn any fibrous food into an exceptionally smooth concoction with a velvety texture.

2. It is versatile

The Nutribullet blender machine is surprisingly versatile. Don't limit its power to just blending smoothies. It can also make delicious dips, sauces, condiments, dressings, soups, ice creams, desserts, and much more. It can also turn nuts into nut butter, wheat berries into wheat flour, and rice into rice flour.

3. There are lots of recipes

The Nutribullet blender is turning out one of the trendiest kitchen gadgets and you can find plenty of recipes that can make you excited for its wonderful use in your kitchen. The standard package of Nutribullet blender comes with a user guide and recipe book, packed with super-nutritious recipes. Plus, you don't have to just stick with only Nutribullet recipes. You can practically use any blending recipe you like.

4. It is very affordable

The most compelling advantage of buying this blender is its reasonable price. Its price won't break your wallet, and it's powerful enough to turn out anything smooth.

Common Pantry Ingredients for Blending

Making a meal from scratch and with fresh ingredients used to be a time-consuming and exhausting task, but not anymore. With smart meal prepping by using shelf-stable ingredients, making your favorite food becomes easy. The following are some must-have pantry items that make preparing meals more convenient and enjoyable.

- Frozen vegetables and fruits

Frozen produce, from spinach to sweet corn to berries, is one of the best things that you can stock in your pantry from the grocery store. Plus, they are convenient, affordable, and nutritious.

- Nuts

Nuts are often used as a snack only, but you can use them in multiple ways in the kitchen. They can be used to make nut milk or nut butter. Furthermore, you can use the blended nut butter and milk in whipping up a smoothie or even a homemade latte. A scoop of nut butter adds bold flavors and texture in sauces and stir-fry dishes. They also elevate taste in baking and cooking.

- Seeds

Seeds are plant-based proteins and offer a significant dose of healthy nutrients. You can reap its benefits by adding into your smoothie bowls or sprinkle them on top of yogurt or salads. Also, both nuts and seeds are the least expensive ones, and you feel good about what you eat for your body.

- Dried Fruits

Dry fruits like dates, raisins, cranberries, and apricot are an excellent nutrient-rich snack. They add natural sweetness, fiber, and anti-inflammatory benefits to the recipes.

Add pitted dates into your smoothies instead of sugar, top raisins over the oatmeal bowl, stir chopped dried apricots in yogurt, or just enjoy them as a snack. You can also pulse dried fruits with your favorites into a jam.

- Beans

Canned beans, like chickpeas, pinto beans, and black beans, offer a mighty dose of nutrients. They are packed with fiber, vitamins, and minerals. You can use them to make a quick dip like hummus or add them in your soups, salads, or side dishes. Just make sure to drain them and rinse properly prior to use.

- Whole Grains

Grains are rich in carbs and, thus, have a bad reputation. But intake of grains like oats, quinoa, and rice are actually linked to long life and better health. Start your day on a healthy note with oats in breakfast or use grains as a base for stir-fry foods.

- Tomatoes

Canned tomatoes are loaded with antioxidants that help the body from several chronic diseases. Fresh ripe tomatoes are perishable, but canned tomatoes work as a good substitute. You can use canned tomatoes to make sauces for pizza or paste, like marinara sauce.

- Broth

Keeping broths like vegetables, chicken, or beef on hand is very useful for making sauces, soups, and poaching meats and vegetables. They are also handy in whipping up soups in your Nutribullet blender. For this, you can use some on hand or frozen veggies and broth to blend up a smoothest and filling soup.

How to Clean NutriBullet Blender?

The Nutribullet blender doesn't require self-cleaning. It is effortless to clean. There are two ways to clean your NutriBullet blender – dishwashing it or cleaning on your own. The jar and lid are dishwasher safe, and the top rack of any dishwasher can be used for this job. Of course, in case of the unavailability of a dishwasher, you can also hand wash the blender with warm soapy water. Cleaning a NutriBullet blender is much easier if you do it right after you have used it. But, if you can't wash it immediately, you should at least fill its jar with soapy water to soak. Here's how you can clean your blender the right way.

- Once you are done using the blender, fill the blender jar halfway with warm water and then add few drops of dishwashing soap. Then cover the jar with its lid and blend on low speed for 1 minute. After this, pour the soapy mixture into the sink and then rinse the jar until clean.

- If you see any stains in the jar, add some chopped lemon or white vinegar before blending the soap mixture. This should wash out the stains, and the lemon gives a pleasant smell to the jar.

- If there are stubborn stains in the jar, remove them by using a toothbrush or a rough sponge. After this, pour in a bit of warm water into it along with dish soap and then blend until stains disappear completely.

- If your blender is very dirty, soak it overnight. For this, pour 1 cup of white vinegar into the jar, add few drops of liquid dish wash and then add ½ cup of baking soda. The mixture will start bubbling, so wait until the bubbles subside and then blend the mixture. After this, let jar soak for a minimum of 6 hours or overnight and then pour out the mixture. Rinse the jar until completely clean, and it gives off the smell of vinegar or baking soda, consider doing the blending of dishwashing soap and water.

- After you have cleaned the inside of the blending jar, separate the jar and blade and dry the inside of the jar. For this, leave the jar upside-down on a drying rack.
- The blender blade is still dirty after blending dishwashing soap and cleaning the jar. Unscrew the blades from the jug, remove any tough bits by scrubbing with a toothbrush and then hand wash it by using hot water and dish soap.
- If you don't want to remove the blade, you can also clean them in the jug. For this, cover the blade by pouring in hot water, then add two tablets of polident and let soak for 30 minutes.
- In the meantime, you can clean the blending machine or base. Soak a towel or sponge in warm soapy water until just damp and then gently run it over the machine to clean off the dirty spots on it. You cannot wash the machine or base as it contains the control system and electronic motor for the appliance. And, these parts should not be exposed to moisture. Just like the jar, it is better to clean the base/machine before it dries, or else cleaning the surface will be more difficult.

Chapter 2: Power Boosting Smoothie

Avocado and Berry Smoothie

Preparation time: 5 minutes

Cooking time: 0 minute

Servings: 2

Ingredients:

- 2 cups almond milk, unsweetened
- ¼ cup mixed berries
- 1 cup mixed greens
- ¼ of avocado, pitted
- 1 teaspoon lime juice
- 1 tablespoon flaxseeds
- 3 tablespoons vanilla flavored protein powder
- 2/3 cup ice cubes

Method:

1. Plug in and switch on the NutriBullet blender and then add all the ingredients in the order into the jar.
2. Cover with the lid, press 'high', then press 'pulse' and let the ingredients blend until incorporated and smooth.
3. Divide smoothie between two glasses and then serve.

Nutrition Value:

- Calories: 295 Cal

- Fat: 17 g
- Carbs: 22.6 g
- Protein: 17.2 g
- Fiber: 9.4 g

Banana Cherry Powder Smoothie

Preparation time: 5 minutes

Cooking time: 0 minute

Servings: 2

Ingredients:

- 2 cups almond milk, unsweetened
- 2 bananas, peeled
- 2/3 cup frozen cherries
- 2 tablespoons vanilla flavored protein powder

Method:

1. Plug in and switch on the NutriBullet blender and then add all the ingredients in the order into the jar.
2. Cover with the lid, press 'high', then press 'pulse' and let the ingredients blend until incorporated and smooth.
3. Divide smoothie between two glasses and then serve.

Nutrition Value:

- Calories: 258 Cal
- Fat: 5.4 g
- Carbs: 45.4 g
- Protein: 11 g
- Fiber: 6 g

Cashew and Banana Smoothie

Preparation time: 5 minutes

Cooking time: 0 minute

Servings: 2

Ingredients:

- 1 ½ cup almond milk, unsweetened
- 1 cup spinach
- ¾ cup strawberries
- ½ of avocado
- 1 ¼ tablespoon cashew butter
- ½ of banana
- 2 tablespoons vanilla protein powder

Method:

1. Plug in and switch on the NutriBullet blender and then add all the ingredients in the order into the jar.
2. Cover with the lid, press 'high', then press 'pulse' and let the ingredients blend until incorporated and smooth.
3. Divide smoothie between two glasses and then serve.

Nutrition Value:

- Calories: 441.6 Cal
- Fat: 26.5 g
- Carbs: 42.7 g
- Protein: 16.5 g
- Fiber: 11.4 g

Strawberry and Walnut Smoothie

Preparation time: 5 minutes

Cooking time: 0 minute

Servings: 2

Ingredients:

- 1 ½ cup almond milk, unsweetened
- 1 cup spinach
- 1 cup strawberries
- ¼ of avocado
- ½ teaspoon ground cinnamon
- 1 tablespoon walnuts
- 2 tablespoons vanilla protein powder
- 1 teaspoon flax seeds
- ½ cup ice cubes

Method:

1. Plug in and switch on the NutriBullet blender and then add all the ingredients in the order into the jar.
2. Cover with the lid, press 'high', then press 'pulse' and let the ingredients blend until incorporated and smooth.
3. Divide smoothie between two glasses and then serve.

Nutrition Value:

- Calories: 286.1 Cal
- Fat: 16.6 g

- Carbs: 26.3 g
- Protein: 13.5 g
- Fiber: 9.7 g

Cinnamon Toast Smoothie

Preparation time: 5 minutes

Cooking time: 0 minute

Servings: 2

Ingredients:

- 1 ½ cup almond milk, unsweetened
- 1 ½ cup baby kale
- ½ teaspoon ground cinnamon
- 2 tablespoons almonds
- 1 banana, peeled
- 1 ½ tablespoon vanilla flavored protein powder
- ½ cup ice cubes

Method:

1. Plug in and switch on the NutriBullet blender and then add all the ingredients in the order into the jar.
2. Cover with the lid, press 'high', then press 'pulse' and let the ingredients blend until incorporated and smooth.
3. Divide smoothie between two glasses and then serve.

Nutrition Value:

- Calories: 312.7 Cal
- Fat: 13.8 g
- Carbs: 38 g
- Protein: 13.2 g
- Fiber: 9.3 g

Choco and Cherry Smoothie

Preparation time: 5 minutes

Cooking time: 0 minute

Servings: 2

Ingredients:

- 1 ½ cup almond milk, unsweetened
- 1 banana
- 1 cup collard greens
- ½ cup frozen cherries
- 2 tablespoons vanilla flavored protein powder
- 1 teaspoon cacao nibs

Method:

1. Plug in and switch on the NutriBullet blender and then add all the ingredients in the order into the jar.
2. Cover with the lid, press 'high', then press 'pulse' and let the ingredients blend until incorporated and smooth.
3. Divide smoothie between two glasses and then serve.

Nutrition Value:

- Calories: 285.9 Cal
- Fat: 6.5 g
- Carbs: 48.7 g
- Protein: 12.1 g
- Fiber: 7.9 g

Apple and Peanut Butter Smoothie

Preparation time: 5 minutes

Cooking time: 0 minute

Servings: 2

Ingredients:

- 1 1/2 cup almond milk, unsweetened
- 1 cup kale
- 1 medium green apple, cored
- ½ of banana
- 1 teaspoon Maca powder
- 1 tablespoon vanilla flavored protein powder
- 1 tablespoon peanut butter, unsalted

Method:

1. Plug in and switch on the NutriBullet blender and then add all the ingredients in the order into the jar.
2. Cover with the lid, press 'high', then press 'pulse' and let the ingredients blend until incorporated and smooth.
3. Divide smoothie between two glasses and then serve.

Nutrition Value:

- Calories: 348.8 Cal
- Fat: 13.2 g
- Carbs: 49.6 g
- Protein: 10.7 g
- Fiber: 8.8 g

Lemon Muffin Smoothie

Preparation time: 5 minutes

Cooking time: 0 minute

Servings: 2

Ingredients:

- 1 1/2 cup almond milk, unsweetened
- 1 cup spinach
- ½ of banana, peeled
- 1/4 cup oats, rolled
- 1/2 teaspoon lemon zest
- 1 tablespoon cashews, unsalted
- 1 teaspoon poppy seeds
- 1 tablespoon vanilla flavored protein powder
- 1 tablespoon lemon juice
- 1/2 teaspoon vanilla extract, unsweetened

Method:

1. Plug in and switch on the NutriBullet blender and then add all the ingredients in the order into the jar.
2. Cover with the lid, press 'high', then press 'pulse' and let the ingredients blend until incorporated and smooth.
3. Divide smoothie between two glasses and then serve.

Nutrition Value:

- Calories: 291.2 Cal

- Fat: 11 g
- Carbs: 39.4 g
- Protein: 11.4 g
- Fiber: 6.3 g

Strawberry Cupcake Smoothie

Preparation time: 5 minutes

Cooking time: 0 minute

Servings: 2

Ingredients:

- 1 ½ cup almond milk, unsweetened
- 2 tablespoons oats, rolled, gluten-free
- 1 1/2 cup spinach
- ½ of banana, peeled
- 1 cup strawberries, frozen
- 1 tablespoon chia seeds
- 2 tablespoons vanilla flavored protein powder

Method:

1. Plug in and switch on the NutriBullet blender and then add all the ingredients in the order into the jar.
2. Cover with the lid, press 'high', then press 'pulse' and let the ingredients blend until incorporated and smooth.
3. Divide smoothie between two glasses and then serve.

Nutrition Value:

- Calories: 320 Cal
- Fat: 10.5 g
- Carbs: 45.7 g
- Protein: 15 g
- Fiber: 45.7 g

Superfood Coffee Smoothie

Preparation time: 5 minutes

Cooking time: 0 minute

Servings: 2

Ingredients:

- 1/2 cup black coffee, cooled
- 1 cup almond milk, unsweetened
- 1 banana, peeled
- 5 strawberries, frozen
- 1 cup spinach
- 1/2 teaspoon ground cinnamon
- 1 tablespoon chocolate flavored Superfood Super boost
- 1 tablespoon coconut oil

Method:

1. Plug in and switch on the NutriBullet blender and then add all the ingredients in the order into the jar.
2. Cover with the lid, press 'high', then press 'pulse' and let the ingredients blend until incorporated and smooth.
3. Divide smoothie between two glasses and then serve.

Nutrition Value:

- Calories: 318.6 Cal
- Fat: 17.3 g
- Carbs: 40.5 g
- Protein: 4.7 g
- Fiber: 7.7 g

Chia, Mango and Berry Smoothie

Preparation time: 5 minutes

Cooking time: 0 minute

Servings: 2

Ingredients:

- 1 cup almond milk, unsweetened
- ½ cup Greek yogurt
- 1 cup frozen raspberries
- 1 cup frozen mango chunks
- 1 teaspoons honey
- 1 tablespoon chia seeds

Method:

1. Plug in and switch on the NutriBullet blender and then add all the ingredients in the order into the jar.
2. Cover with the lid, press 'high', then press 'pulse' and let the ingredients blend until incorporated and smooth.
3. Divide smoothie between two glasses and then serve.

Nutrition Value:

- Calories: 210 Cal
- Fat: 4 g
- Carbs: 32.2 g
- Protein: 9.1 g
- Fiber: 7.4 g

Green Tea and Mixed Fruits Smoothie

Preparation time: 5 minutes

Cooking time: 0 minute

Servings: 2

Ingredients:

- 1 ½ cup green tea
- 2 plums, pitted, halved
- 2 peaches, pitted, quartered
- 2 nectarines, pitted, quartered
- 2 limes, juiced

Method:

1. Plug in and switch on the NutriBullet blender and then add all the ingredients in the order into the jar.
2. Cover with the lid, press 'high', then press 'pulse' and let the ingredients blend until incorporated and smooth.
3. Divide smoothie between two glasses and then serve.

Nutrition Value:

- Calories: 181 Cal
- Fat: 1.2 g
- Carbs: 37.2 g
- Protein: 3.5 g
- Fiber: 7.5 g

Chia Seeds and Coconut Smoothie

Preparation time: 5 minutes

Cooking time: 0 minute

Servings: 2

Ingredients:

- 1 ½ cup almond milk, unsweetened
- 1 cup spinach
- 1 teaspoon coconut butter
- 1 cup mixed berries, frozen
- 1 teaspoon ground turmeric
- 1 teaspoon chia seeds
- 2 1/2 teaspoon chocolate flavored Superfood Super boost

Method:

1. Plug in and switch on the NutriBullet blender and then add all the ingredients in the order into the jar.
2. Cover with the lid, press 'high', then press 'pulse' and let the ingredients blend until incorporated and smooth.
3. Divide smoothie between two glasses and then serve.

Nutrition Value:

- Calories: 228.1 Cal
- Fat: 9.9 g
- Carbs: 29.6 g
- Protein: 5 g
- Fiber: 10.7 g

Carrot Cake Smoothie

Preparation time: 5 minutes

Cooking time: 0 minute

Servings: 2

Ingredients:

- 1 ½ cup almond milk, unsweetened
- ¼ cup Greek yogurt, plain, non-fat
- 1/2 cup diced carrot
- 2 Medjool dates, pitted
- 1/4 teaspoon ground cinnamon
- 1 tablespoon coconut flakes, unsweetened
- 1/8 teaspoon ground nutmeg

Method:

1. Plug in and switch on the NutriBullet blender and then add all the ingredients in the order into the jar.
2. Cover with the lid, press 'high', then press 'pulse' and let the ingredients blend until incorporated and smooth.
3. Divide smoothie between two glasses and then serve.

Nutrition Value:

- Calories: 301.1 Cal
- Fat: 8.7 g
- Carbs: 51.7 g
- Protein: 10 g
- Fiber: 7.1 g

Mango and Avocado Smoothie

Preparation time: 5 minutes

Cooking time: 0 minute

Servings: 2

Ingredients:

- 1 ½ cup coconut water
- 1 cup baby kale
- 1 cup frozen mango chunks
- ¼ of avocado
- 2 tablespoons vanilla flavored protein powder
- 1 tablespoon cashew

Method:

1. Plug in and switch on the NutriBullet blender and then add all the ingredients in the order into the jar.
2. Cover with the lid, press 'high', then press 'pulse' and let the ingredients blend until incorporated and smooth.
3. Divide smoothie between two glasses and then serve.

Nutrition Value:

- Calories: 327.6 Cal
- Fat: 11.7 g
- Carbs: 46.3 g
- Protein: 12.6 g
- Fiber: 6.5 g

Blackberries Smoothie

Preparation time: 5 minutes

Cooking time: 0 minute

Servings: 2

Ingredients:

- 1 cup almond milk, unsweetened
- ½ cup water
- 1 tablespoon almond butter, unsalted
- ½ cup frozen blackberries
- 2 cups spinach
- ½ cup frozen cherries
- ½ tablespoon grated ginger
- 1 teaspoon ground cinnamon
- 2 tablespoons vanilla flavored protein powder
- ½ tablespoon coconut oil

Method:

1. Plug in and switch on the NutriBullet blender and then add all the ingredients in the order into the jar.
2. Cover with the lid, press 'high', then press 'pulse' and let the ingredients blend until incorporated and smooth.
3. Divide smoothie between two glasses and then serve.

Nutrition Value:

- Calories: 371.5 Cal
- Fat: 20.8 g

- Carbs: 35.7 g
- Protein: 15.4 g
- Fiber: 11.4 g

Caramel Apple Smoothie

Preparation time: 5 minutes

Cooking time: 0 minute

Servings: 2

Ingredients:

- ¾ cup almond milk, unsweetened
- 1 tablespoon almond butter, unsalted
- ½ of green apple
- 1 cup spinach
- 1 Medjool date, pitted
- 1 cup kale
- ¾ cup water
- 1/8 teaspoon ground cinnamon
- 2 tablespoons vanilla flavored protein powder
- 1/3 cup ice cubes

Method:

1. Plug in and switch on the NutriBullet blender and then add all the ingredients in the order into the jar.
2. Cover with the lid, press 'high', then press 'pulse' and let the ingredients blend until incorporated and smooth.
3. Divide smoothie between two glasses and then serve.

Nutrition Value:

- Calories: 311.4 Cal

- Fat: 13.2 g
- Carbs: 38.6 g
- Protein: 14 g
- Fiber: 8.6 g

Creamy Pineapple Smoothie

Preparation time: 5 minutes

Cooking time: 0 minute

Servings: 2

Ingredients:

- 1 ½ cup almond milk, unsweetened
- ¼ of medium avocado
- 1 ½ cup spinach
- 1 cup fresh pineapple chunks
- 1 ½ tablespoon vanilla flavored protein powder
- 1 teaspoon flaxseeds
- ½ cup ice cubes

Method:

1. Plug in and switch on the NutriBullet blender and then add all the ingredients in the order into the jar.
2. Cover with the lid, press 'high', then press 'pulse' and let the ingredients blend until incorporated and smooth.
3. Divide smoothie between two glasses and then serve.

Nutrition Value:

- Calories: 273 Cal
- Fat: 13 g
- Carbs: 32.5 g
- Protein: 10.9 g
- Fiber: 8.8 g

Chapter 3: High – Protein Smoothie

Blackberry and Almond Shake

Preparation time: 5 minutes

Cooking time: 0 minute

Servings: 2

Ingredients:

- 1/2 cup coconut milk, canned
- 1 cup water
- 1/2 cup blackberries, frozen
- 2 tablespoons macadamia nuts
- 1 teaspoon hemp seeds
- 1 packet of liquid stevia
- 1/8 teaspoon sea salt
- 1 1/2 tablespoon vanilla flavored protein powder
- 1 teaspoon MCT oil
- 2/3 cup ice cubes

Method:

1. Plug in and switch on the NutriBullet blender and then add all the ingredients in the order into the jar.
2. Cover with the lid, press 'high', then press 'pulse' and let the ingredients blend until incorporated and smooth.
3. Divide smoothie between two glasses and then serve.

Nutrition Value:

- Calories: 490.9 Cal
- Fat: 44.3 g
- Carbs: 19.6 g
- Protein: 11.4 g
- Fiber: 6 g

and Banana Protein Smoothie

Preparation time: 5 minutes

Cooking time: 0 minute

Servings: 2

Ingredients:

- 1 1/2 cup almond milk, unsweetened
- ½ of banana
- 2 tablespoons Greek yogurt
- 1 cup spinach
- 1 cup mixed berries, frozen
- 1/2 teaspoon ground cinnamon
- 2 tablespoons vanilla flavored protein powder
- 1 tablespoon almond butter, no added salt

Method:

1. Plug in and switch on the NutriBullet blender and then add all the ingredients in the order into the jar.
2. Cover with the lid, press 'high', then press 'pulse' and let the ingredients blend until incorporated and smooth.
3. Divide smoothie between two glasses and then serve.

Nutrition Value:

- Calories: 367 Cal
- Fat: 14.8 g
- Carbs: 44.1 g
- Protein: 18.2 g
- Fiber: 11.1 g

Carrot Protein Shake

Preparation time: 5 minutes

Cooking time: 0 minute

Servings: 2

Ingredients:

- 1 1/2 cup almond milk, unsweetened
- 1 cup spinach
- ½ of frozen banana, peeled
- 1 cup baby carrots
- 1 tablespoons raisin, seedless
- 1/8 teaspoon ground nutmeg
- 2 tablespoons vanilla flavored protein powder
- 1/8 teaspoon ground clove
- 1/2 teaspoon ground cinnamon
- 1/3 cup ice cubes

Method:

1. Plug in and switch on the NutriBullet blender and then add all the ingredients in the order into the jar.
2. Cover with the lid, press 'high', then press 'pulse' and let the ingredients blend until incorporated and smooth.
3. Divide shake between two glasses and then serve.

Nutrition Value:

- Calories: 240 Cal

- Fat: 6.7 g
- Carbs: 36.2 g
- Protein: 11.8 g
- Fiber: 8.8 g

Grape Protein Smoothie

Preparation time: 5 minutes

Cooking time: 0 minute

Servings: 2

Ingredients:

- 3 cups almond milk, unsweetened
- 1 banana, peeled
- 2 cups spinach
- 4 tablespoons orange juice
- 2 cups grapes
- 2 tablespoons dried goji berries
- 2 tablespoons vanilla flavored protein powder
- ½ cup frozen green peas

Method:

1. Plug in and switch on the NutriBullet blender and then add all the ingredients in the order into the jar.
2. Cover with the lid, press 'high', then press 'pulse' and let the ingredients blend until incorporated and smooth.
3. Divide smoothie between two glasses and then serve.

Nutrition Value:

- Calories: 304.2 Cal
- Fat: 5 g
- Carbs: 60.1 g
- Protein: 10.7 g
- Fiber: 7 g

Muesli Smoothie

Preparation time: 5 minutes

Cooking time: 0 minute

Servings: 2

Ingredients:

- 1 cup almond milk, unsweetened
- 1 medium green apple, cored
- 1/2 cup rolled oats
- 1 banana, peeled
- 1 teaspoon ground cinnamon
- ¼ cup roasted pecans, unsalted
- 2 tablespoons vanilla flavored protein powder

Method:

1. Plug in and switch on the NutriBullet blender and then add all the ingredients in the order into the jar.
2. Cover with the lid, press 'high', then press 'pulse' and let the ingredients blend until incorporated and smooth.
3. Divide smoothie between two glasses and then serve.

Nutrition Value:

- Calories: 675.1 Cal
- Fat: 23.5 g
- Carbs: 97.4 g
- Protein: 25.8 g
- Fiber: 16.3 g

Green Protein Smoothie

Preparation time: 5 minutes

Cooking time: 0 minute

Servings: 2

Ingredients:

- 1 1/2 cup almond milk, unsweetened
- ½ of banana, peeled
- 1/2 cup Greek yogurt
- 2 cups spinach
- 1 tablespoon peanut butter, unsalted
- 1/2 teaspoon ground cinnamon
- 1 tablespoon vanilla flavored protein powder

Method:

1. Plug in and switch on the NutriBullet blender and then add all the ingredients in the order into the jar.
2. Cover with the lid, press 'high', then press 'pulse' and let the ingredients blend until incorporated and smooth.
3. Divide smoothie between two glasses and then serve.

Nutrition Value:

- Calories: 322.7 Cal
- Fat: 13.4 g
- Carbs: 31 g
- Protein: 24.5 g
- Fiber: 5.4 g

kin Spice Protein Smoothie

Preparation time: 5 minutes

Cooking time: 0 minute

Servings: 2

Ingredients:

- 1 1/2 cup almond milk, unsweetened
- 1/3 cup pumpkin puree
- 1 tablespoon almond butter, unsalted
- 1 banana, peeled
- 1/4 teaspoon pumpkin spice
- 2 tablespoons vanilla flavored protein powder
- 1/2 cup ice cubes

Method:

1. Plug in and switch on the NutriBullet blender and then add all the ingredients in the order into the jar.
2. Cover with the lid, press 'high', then press 'pulse' and let the ingredients blend until incorporated and smooth.
3. Divide smoothie between two glasses and then serve.

Nutrition Value:

- Calories: 346.8 Cal
- Fat: 15.7 g
- Carbs: 42 g
- Protein: 15.3 g
- Fiber: 10.3 g

Strawberry Protein Punch

Preparation time: 5 minutes

Cooking time: 0 minute

Servings: 2

Ingredients:

- 1/2 cup almond milk, unsweetened
- 2 cups kale
- 1 cup water
- 1 cup frozen strawberries
- 1 1/2 tablespoon cashew butter, unsalted
- 1/2 cup frozen cherries
- 1 tablespoon rolled oats, rolled, gluten-free
- 1/4 teaspoon vanilla extract, unsweetened
- 2 tablespoons vanilla flavored protein powder

Method:

1. Plug in and switch on the NutriBullet blender and then add all the ingredients in the order into the jar.
2. Cover with the lid, press 'high', then press 'pulse' and let the ingredients blend until incorporated and smooth.
3. Divide smoothie between two glasses and then serve.

Nutrition Value:

- Calories: 346.1 Cal
- Fat: 16 g

- Carbs: 40 g
- Protein: 15.2 g
- Fiber: 8.2 g

Zucchini, Avocado and Almond Smoothie

Preparation time: 5 minutes

Cooking time: 0 minute

Servings: 2

Ingredients:

- 1 1/2 cup almond milk, unsweetened
- 1 tablespoon almond butter
- ½ of banana
- 1/2 cup fresh zucchini
- 1 teaspoon cacao nibs
- ½ of avocado
- 1/2 tablespoon cacao powder
- 2 tablespoons vanilla flavored protein powder
- 2/3 cup ice cubes

Method:

1. Plug in and switch on the NutriBullet blender and then add all the ingredients in the order into the jar.
2. Cover with the lid, press 'high', then press 'pulse' and let the ingredients blend until incorporated and smooth.
3. Divide smoothie between two glasses and then serve.

Nutrition Value:

- Calories: 419.3 Cal
- Fat: 26.5 g

- Carbs: 35.4 g
- Protein: 16.3 g
- Fiber: 12 g

Pumpkin Pie Protein Smoothie

Preparation time: 5 minutes

Cooking time: 0 minute

Servings: 2

Ingredients:

- 1 1/2 cup almond milk, unsweetened
- ½ of banana
- 1/4 cup pumpkin puree
- 1/2 cup peach, pitted
- 1/2 teaspoon ground cinnamon
- 1/2 cup fresh pineapple chunks
- 1/2 teaspoon ground allspice
- 1 tablespoon vanilla flavored protein powder

Method:

1. Plug in and switch on the NutriBullet blender and then add all the ingredients in the order into the jar.
2. Cover with the lid, press 'high', then press 'pulse' and let the ingredients blend until incorporated and smooth.
3. Divide smoothie between two glasses and then serve.

Nutrition Value:

- Calories: 230.8 Cal
- Fat: 5.1 g
- Carbs: 43.9 g
- Protein: 8.2 g
- Fiber: 8.3 g

Chapter 4: Green Smoothie

Skinny Green Smoothie

Preparation time: 5 minutes

Cooking time: 0 minute

Servings: 2

Ingredients:

- 1 cup almond milk, unsweetened
- 1 cup spinach
- ½ of medium cucumber
- ½ cup coconut water
- ½ cup parsley
- 1 medium green apple, cored
- 1 tablespoon coconut oil
- 5 mint leaves
- 1 tablespoon SuperFood Super Boost

Method:

1. Plug in and switch on the NutriBullet blender and then add all the ingredients in the order into the jar.
2. Cover with the lid, press 'high', then press 'pulse' and let the ingredients blend until incorporated and smooth.
3. Divide smoothie between two glasses and then serve.

Nutrition Value:

- Calories: 343.2 Cal
- Fat: 17.1 g
- Carbs: 44.5 g
- Protein: 5.2 g
- Fiber: 9 g

Banana Kale Smoothie

Preparation time: 5 minutes

Cooking time: 0 minute

Servings: 2

Ingredients:

- 1 1/2 cup water
- 1 banana, peeled
- 1 cup kale
- 1/2 cup frozen mixed berries
- 1 tablespoon hemp seeds
- 2 teaspoons SuperFood Super Boost

Method:

1. Plug in and switch on the NutriBullet blender and then add all the ingredients in the order into the jar.
2. Cover with the lid, press 'high', then press 'pulse' and let the ingredients blend until incorporated and smooth.
3. Divide smoothie between two glasses and then serve.

Nutrition Value:

- Calories: 228.5 Cal
- Fat: 6.1 g
- Carbs: 41.6 g
- Protein: 6 g
- Fiber: 7.8 g

Blueberry Yogurt Smoothie

Preparation time: 5 minutes

Cooking time: 0 minute

Servings: 2

Ingredients:

- 1 1/2 cup almond milk, unsweetened
- 1 cup blueberries
- 1/2 cup Greek yogurt
- 1 cup kale
- 1/2 tablespoon grated ginger
- 1 tablespoon lemon juice
- 1 tablespoon SuperFood Super Boost

Method:

1. Plug in and switch on the NutriBullet blender and then add all the ingredients in the order into the jar.
2. Cover with the lid, press 'high', then press 'pulse' and let the ingredients blend until incorporated and smooth.
3. Divide smoothie between two glasses and then serve.

Nutrition Value:

- Calories: 259.6 Cal
- Fat: 5.3 g
- Carbs: 39.7 g
- Protein: 17.1 g
- Fiber: 6.7 g

Chia and Zucchini Smoothie

Preparation time: 5 minutes

Cooking time: 0 minute

Servings: 2

Ingredients:

- 1 ½ cup almond milk, unsweetened
- 1 cup zucchini, fresh
- 1 tablespoon almond butter, unsalted
- 1 tablespoon chia seeds
- 1 teaspoon turmeric powder
- 1/4 teaspoon ground cinnamon
- 3 tablespoons vanilla flavored protein powder
- 2/3 cup ice cubes

Method:

1. Plug in and switch on the NutriBullet blender and then add all the ingredients in the order into the jar.
2. Cover with the lid, press 'high', then press 'pulse' and let the ingredients blend until incorporated and smooth.
3. Divide smoothie between two glasses and then serve.

Nutrition Value:

- Calories: 306.5 Cal
- Fat: 18.3 g
- Carbs: 20.4 g
- Protein: 19.6 g
- Fiber: 8.6 g

Tropic Smoothie

Preparation time: 5 minutes

Cooking time: 0 minute

Servings: 2

Ingredients:

- 1 cup coconut water
- ¼ of medium cucumber
- ½ cup fresh pineapple chunks
- 1 cup spinach
- 5 mint leaves
- 1 tablespoon chia seeds
- ½ tablespoon lime juice
- 1 tablespoon vanilla flavored protein powder

Method:

1. Plug in and switch on the NutriBullet blender and then add all the ingredients in the order into the jar.
2. Cover with the lid, press 'high', then press 'pulse' and let the ingredients blend until incorporated and smooth.
3. Divide smoothie between two glasses and then serve.

Nutrition Value:

- Calories: 180.1 Cal
- Fat: 4.3 g
- Carbs: 30.6 g
- Protein: 7.8 g
- Fiber: 6.1 g

Apple and Tofu Smoothie

Preparation time: 5 minutes

Cooking time: 0 minute

Servings: 2

Ingredients:

- 1 cup almond milk, unsweetened
- 2 cups Swiss chard
- ½ cup coconut water
- 1 medium red apple, cored
- ½ cup tofu, firm
- 2 tablespoons rolled oats
- 1 tablespoon almond butter, unsalted
- ½ teaspoon ground cinnamon
- 2 tablespoons vanilla flavored protein powder

Method:

1. Plug in and switch on the NutriBullet blender and then add all the ingredients in the order into the jar.
2. Cover with the lid, press 'high', then press 'pulse' and let the ingredients blend until incorporated and smooth.
3. Divide smoothie between two glasses and then serve.

Nutrition Value:

- Calories: 444.1 Cal
- Fat: 17.7 g

- Carbs: 51.5 g
- Protein: 22.7 g
- Fiber: 11.3 g

Citrus Smoothie

Preparation time: 5 minutes

Cooking time: 0 minute

Servings: 2

Ingredients:

- 1 cup coconut water
- 2 cups kale
- ½ cup water
- ¼ cup cucumber pieces
- 1 orange
- 1 tablespoon lemon juice
- 1 teaspoon honey
- 1 teaspoon superfood essential greens

Method:

1. Plug in and switch on the NutriBullet blender and then add all the ingredients in the order into the jar.
2. Cover with the lid, press 'high', then press 'pulse' and let the ingredients blend until incorporated and smooth.
3. Divide smoothie between two glasses and then serve.

Nutrition Value:

- Calories: 152 Cal
- Fat: 0.7 g
- Carbs: 36.6 g
- Protein: 3 g
- Fiber: 5.3 g

Herbal Smoothie

Preparation time: 5 minutes

Cooking time: 0 minute

Servings: 2

Ingredients:

- 1 1/2 cup water
- 3 cups Swiss Chard
- ¾ cup frozen blueberries
- 1 tablespoon cilantro leaves
- 1/4 cup roasted cashews, unsalted
- 1 tablespoon mint leaves
- 2 teaspoons superfood essential greens
- ½ tablespoon lime juice

Method:

1. Plug in and switch on the NutriBullet blender and then add all the ingredients in the order into the jar.
2. Cover with the lid, press 'high', then press 'pulse' and let the ingredients blend until incorporated and smooth.
3. Divide smoothie between two glasses and then serve.

Nutrition Value:

- Calories: 292.6 Cal
- Fat: 17 g
- Carbs: 33.5 g
- Protein: 7.8 g
- Fiber: 7.4 g

...ancakes

Preparation time: 5 minutes

Cooking time: 8 minutes

Servings: 4

Ingredients:

- 1 small white onion, peeled, halved
- 2 eggs, room temperature
- 2 tablespoons all-purpose flour
- 1/8 teaspoon cayenne pepper
- ½ teaspoon salt
- 2 medium potatoes, peeled, 1-inch cubed
- 2 tablespoons olive oil

Method:

1. Plug in and switch on the NutriBullet blender and then add onion and eggs into the jar.
2. Cover with the lid, press 'high', press 'pulse' until blended, then add potatoes and continue processing until chopped.
3. Tip the mixture into a medium bowl, add flour in it and then stir in salt and cayenne pepper until well combined.
4. Take a medium skillet pan, add 2 tablespoons oil in it and when hot, drop pancake batter into it.

5. Spread the batter evenly to shape pancake and then fry for 2 to 3 minutes per side until golden brown and cooked.

6. Transfer pancakes to a plate lined with paper towels and then serve.

Nutrition Value:

- Calories: 263 Cal
- Fat: 17 g
- Carbs: 23 g
- Protein: 6 g
- Fiber: 3 g

Cream Soup

Time: 5 minutes

Cooking time: 15 minutes

Servings: 4

Ingredients:

- ½ of medium white onion, peeled, sliced
- 1 ½ cup canned chickpeas
- 1 tablespoon minced garlic
- 1 teaspoon grated ginger
- ½ teaspoon sea salt
- 1/8 teaspoon ground nutmeg
- ¼ teaspoon ground black pepper
- 1/8 teaspoon ground clove
- 1 tablespoon unsalted butter
- 1 tablespoon olive oil
- 2 cups vegetable broth
- 2 cups pumpkin puree
- ½ cup heavy cream

Method:

1. Take a medium pot, place it over medium heat, add oil and butter and when butter melts, add onion, chickpeas and garlic, stir and cook for 3 to 4 minutes until softened.

2. Then add all the spices, stir until mixed, then remove pot from heat and let it cool for 10 minutes.

3. Transfer chickpeas mixture into the NutriBullet blender and then add remaining ingredients into the jar except for cream.

4. Plug in and switch on the blender, cover with the lid, and then press 'high', then press 'pulse' for 30 until smooth mixture comes together.

5. Pour the soup into the pot, stir in cream until well combined, return pot over medium heat and let the soup simmer for 10 minutes until thick and hot.

6. When done, ladle soup into bowls and then serve.

Nutrition Value:

- Calories: 292 Cal
- Fat: 19.1 g
- Carbs: 26.3 g
- Protein: 7.2 g
- Fiber: 9 g

...nd Beet Soup

...ne: 10 minutes

Cooking time: 45 minutes

Servings: 2

Ingredients:

- 2 medium beets, peeled, chopped
- ¼ of a medium white onion, peeled, chopped
- 3 ½ small red potatoes, peeled, chopped
- ½ teaspoon ground cinnamon
- ¼ teaspoon sea salt
- ¼ teaspoon ground nutmeg
- ¼ teaspoon ground black pepper
- 2 teaspoons olive oil
- 1 cup pumpkin puree
- 2 tablespoons pumpkin seeds, unsalted
- ½ cup coconut milk, unsweetened
- 1 ½ cup water

Method:

1. Switch on the oven, then set it to 400 degrees F and let it preheat.
2. Then take a baking tray, line it with foil, spread onion, potatoes and beet pieces on it, season with salt and drizzle with oil.
3. Toss well until all the vegetables are coated with oil and salt and then bake for 35 minutes until softened.

4. When done, let the vegetables cool for 15 to 20 minutes and then transfer then into the NutriBullet blender.

5. Plug in and switch on the blender, add remaining ingredients into the jar, cover with the lid, press 'high', then press 'pulse' for 40 to 50 seconds until smooth.

6. Pour the soup into the pot, place pot over medium heat and let the soup simmer for 10 minutes until thick and hot.

7. When done, ladle soup into bowls and then serve.

Nutrition Value:

- Calories: 386.9 Cal
- Fat: 10.5 g
- Carbs: 67.7 g
- Protein: 11.4 g
- Fiber: 13.8 g

Broccoli Cheese Soup

Preparation time: 5 minutes

Cooking time: 15 minutes

Servings: 2

Ingredients:

- 3 cups broccoli florets, chopped
- 2 cups almond milk, unsweetened
- 2 teaspoons diced white onion
- 1 cup shredded cheddar cheese, low-fat
- 1 bouillon cube

Method:

1. Take a large heatproof bowl, place broccoli florets in it, cover with a plastic wrap and then microwave for 5 to 8 minutes until tender.
2. Drain the broccoli, transfer them into the NutriBullet blender and then add remaining ingredients.
3. Plug in and switch on the blender, cover with the lid, press 'high', then press 'pulse' for 1 minute until smooth.
4. Pour the soup into the pot, place pot over medium heat and let the soup simmer for 10 minutes until thick and hot.
5. When done, ladle soup into bowls and then serve.

Nutrition Value:

- Calories: 130 Cal
- Fat: 2.5 g

- Carbs: 15 g
- Protein: 14 g
- Fiber: 4 g

Cauliflower Mac and Cheese

Preparation time: 10 minutes

Cooking time: 15 minutes

Servings: 5

Ingredients:

- ¼ cup cauliflower florets, chopped
- 1 ½ cup macaroni noodles, cooked
- 1 cup shredded cheddar cheese
- 2 tablespoons unsalted butter, softened
- ¼ cup ricotta cheese
- 2 tablespoons whole milk

Method:

1. Take a large heatproof bowl, place cauliflower florets in it, cover with a plastic wrap and then microwave for 5 to 8 minutes until tender.
2. Drain the cauliflower, let it cool for 15 minutes, then transfer into the NutriBullet blender and pour in milk.
3. Plug in and switch on the NutriBullet blender, cover with the lid, press 'high', then press 'pulse' until smoot, then add cheeses and butter and pulse again until blended.
4. Pour the sauce into the pot, place pot over medium heat and simmer for 5 minutes until hot.
5. Add cooked macaroni into the pot, toss until coated and continue cooking for 2 minutes until thoroughly warm.
6. Serve straight away.

Nutrition Value:

- Calories: 292.3 Cal
- Fat: 14.2 g
- Carbs: 29.2 g
- Protein: 11.7 g
- Fiber: 1.3 g

Overnight Oats

Preparation time: 5 minutes

Cooking time: 0 minute

Servings: 6

Ingredients:

- 5 cups almond milk, unsweetened
- 2 cups coconut water
- 3 cups rolled oats
- ¼ cup chia seeds
- 1 cup Greek yogurt
- 2 cups strawberries
- 2 tablespoons ground cinnamon
- 2 tablespoons agave nectar
- 2 tablespoons vanilla extract, unsweetened

Method:

1. Take a large bowl, pour in milk and water, add oats and chia seeds and stir until combined.
2. Plug in and switch on the NutriBullet blender and then add remaining ingredients in the order into the jar.
3. Cover with the lid, press 'high', then press 'pulse' and let the ingredients blend until incorporated and smooth.
4. Transfer the blended mixture into the bowl containing oats mixture, stir until combined, cover the bowl with its lid and refrigerate for a minimum of 8 hours.

5. When done, distribute oats evenly among bowls, garnish with favorite toppings and then serve.

Nutrition Value:

- Calories: 312.8 Cal
- Fat: 7.1 g
- Carbs: 49.5 g
- Protein: 12.3 g
- Fiber: 9.3 g

Sweet Potato Pie

Preparation time: 10 minutes

Cooking time: 60 minutes

Servings: 8

Ingredients:

For the Crust:

- 1 cup unroasted pecans and more for topping
- 1 cup unsalted walnuts and more for topping
- 1 cup Medjool dates, pitted

For the Filling:

- 1 cup coconut milk, unsweetened
- 2 sweet potato, roasted, cooled, peeled
- 1 tablespoon vanilla extract, unsweetened
- 1 teaspoon maple syrup
- 1/8 teaspoon sea salt
- ½ teaspoon ground cinnamon

Method:

1. Switch on the oven, then set it to 350 degrees F and let it preheat.
2. Prepare the crust and for this, plug in and switch on the NutriBullet blender and then add pecans and nuts into the jar.
3. Cover with the lid, press 'high', press 'pulse' until ingredients have crumbled and then transfer the nut mixture into a small bowl.

4. Add dates into the blender jar, cover with the lid, press 'high', press 'pulse' until dates are broken and then transfer into the bowl containing nuts mixture and stir until combined.

5. Take a springform pan, place nuts-dates mixture in it and then spread it evenly in the bottom of the pan, pressing firmly.

6. Prepare the filling and for this, place all of its ingredients into the jar of the NutriBullet blender, cover with the lid, press 'high', and then press 'pulse' until smooth.

7. Pour the filling into the prepared crust and then bake into the heated oven for 1 hour until set.

8. When done, top the pie with walnuts and pecans and serve its slice with a dollop of whipped cream.

Nutrition Value:

- Calories: 294.5 Cal
- Fat: 19.1 g
- Carbs: 30.2 g
- Protein: 4.7 g
- Fiber: 5.4 g

Pumpkin Cheesecake

Preparation time: 10 minutes

Cooking time: 0 minute

Servings: 8

Ingredients:

For the Crust:

- 1 cup unroasted pecans and more for topping
- 1 cup unsalted walnuts and more for topping
- 1 cup Medjool dates, pitted

For the Filling:

- ½ cup coconut milk, unsweetened
- ½ cup pumpkin puree
- 2 cups cashews, soaked in hot water for 1 hour
- 1/8 teaspoon sea salt
- ¼ teaspoon ground cinnamon
- 2 tablespoons lemon juice
- ¼ teaspoon pumpkin spice
- ½ cup maple syrup
- 1 teaspoon vanilla extract, unsweetened
- 3 tablespoons coconut oil

Method:

1. Prepare the crust and for this, plug in and switch on the NutriBullet blender and then add pecans and nuts into the jar.

2. Cover with the lid, press 'high', press 'pulse' until ingredients have crumbled and then transfer the nut mixture into a small bowl.

3. Add dates into the blender jar, cover with the lid, press 'high', press 'pulse' until dates are broken and then transfer into the bowl containing nuts mixture and stir until combined.

4. Take a springform pan, place nuts-dates mixture in it and then spread it evenly in the bottom of the pan, pressing firmly.

5. Prepare the filling and for this, drain the cashews, add then into the jar of the NutriBullet blender along with remaining ingredients, cover with the lid, press 'high', and then press 'pulse' until smooth.

6. Pour the filling into the prepared crust, spread it evenly, smooth the top by using a spatula and let it freeze for a minimum of 4 hours until pie is set.

7. When done, top the pie with walnuts and pecans and serve its slice with a dollop of whipped cream.

Nutrition Value:

- Calories: 572.1 Cal
- Fat: 41.7 g
- Carbs: 47.8 g
- Protein: 10.5 g
- Fiber: 5.3 g

Cookie Dough

Preparation time: 10 minutes

Cooking time: 0 minute

Servings: 12

Ingredients:

- 15 ounces canned chickpeas
- 2 tablespoons almond milk
- ¼ teaspoon salt
- 3 tablespoons coconut sugar
- 1 teaspoon vanilla extract, unsweetened
- 1 tablespoon maple syrup
- ¼ cup sunflower seed butter, unsweetened
- ¼ cup mini chocolate chips

Method:

1. Plug in and switch on the NutriBullet blender and then add all the ingredients in the order into the jar except for chocolate chips.
2. Cover with the lid, press 'high', then press 'pulse' and let the ingredients blend until incorporated and smooth.
3. Transfer the mixture into a freezer proof bowl, fold in chocolate chips, then cover with a lid and let it freeze for a minimum of 15 minutes until thoroughly chilled.
4. When ready to eat, spoon dough into a bowl and then serve it with favorite toping.

Nutrition Value:

- Calories: 93 Cal

- Fat: 4 g
- Carbs: 11 g
- Protein: 3 g
- Fiber: 2 g

Brownie-tini

Preparation time: 5 minutes

Cooking time: 0 minute

Servings: 4

Ingredients:

- 1 cup vodka
- 1 cup half-and-half
- 1 cup crumbled baked brownies
- ½ cup Irish cream liqueur
- ½ cup ice cubes
- Grated chocolate, as needed for garnish

Method:

1. Plug in and switch on the NutriBullet blender and then add all the ingredients in the order into the jar, except for chocolate.
2. Cover with the lid, press 'high', then press 'pulse' and let the ingredients blend until incorporated and smooth.
3. Divide martini evenly among four chilled glasses, top with grated chocolate and then serve.

Nutrition Value:

- Calories: 353 Cal
- Fat: 20.8 g
- Carbs: 35.3 g
- Protein: 6.2 g
- Fiber: 3.2 g

Banana Fudge Ice Cream

Preparation time: 5 minutes

Cooking time: 0 minute

Servings: 2

Ingredients:

- 2 frozen bananas, sliced
- 6 ounces firm tofu
- 4 tablespoons cocoa powder, unsweetened
- ½ cup peanut butter powder
- 1 teaspoon chocolate chips
- 10 peanuts, chopped

Method:

1. Plug in and switch on the NutriBullet blender and then banana, tofu, cocoa powder and peanut butter powder into the jar.
2. Cover with the lid, press 'high', then press 'pulse' and let the ingredients blend until incorporated and smooth.
3. Divide ice cream between two bowls, top with chocolate chips and peanuts and then serve.

Nutrition Value:

- Calories: 290 Cal
- Fat: 9 g
- Carbs: 46 g
- Protein: 22 g
- Fiber: 12 g

Strawberry and Almond Dessert Smoothie

Preparation time: 5 minutes

Cooking time: 0 minute

Servings: 2

Ingredients:

- 3 cups almond milk, unsweetened
- 2 frozen bananas
- ½ cup almonds
- 3 cups fresh strawberries
- 10 mint leaves
- 1 teaspoon ground cinnamon
- 2 tablespoons chia seeds
- 2 tablespoons vanilla flavored protein powder
- 2 tablespoons coconut oil

Method:

1. Plug in and switch on the NutriBullet blender and then add all the ingredients in the order into the jar.
2. Cover with the lid, press 'high', then press 'pulse' and let the ingredients blend until incorporated and smooth.
3. Divide smoothie between two glasses and then serve.

Nutrition Value:

- Calories: 594.4 Cal
- Fat: 37 g

- Carbs: 57.8 g
- Protein: 15.7 g
- Fiber: 16.4 g

Chilled Raspberry Soup

Preparation time: 5 minutes

Cooking time: 0 minute

Servings: 2

Ingredients:

- ½ cup cranberry juice cocktail
- 8 cups raspberries and more for topping
- 1 cup coconut sugar
- 2 cups sour cream

Method:

1. Plug in and switch on the NutriBullet blender and then add cocktail, berries and sugar into the jar.
2. Cover with the lid, press 'high', then press 'pulse' and let the ingredients blend until incorporated and smooth.
3. Transfer the mixture into a large bowl, add sour cream and then stir until combined.
4. Cover the bowl with a lid, then refrigerate for a minimum of 2 hours until thoroughly chilled.
5. Garnish soup with more raspberries and then serve.

Nutrition Value:

- Calories: 160 Cal
- Fat: 8 g
- Carbs: 28 g
- Protein: 2 g
- Fiber: 6 g

Strawberry and Watermelon Slush

Preparation time: 5 minutes

Cooking time: 0 minute

Servings: 4

Ingredients:

- 2 cups seedless watermelon chunks
- 1/3 cup lemon juice
- 2 cups fresh strawberries, halved
- 1/3 cup coconut sugar
- 2 cups ice cubes

Method:

1. Plug in and switch on the NutriBullet blender and then add all the ingredients in the order into the jar except for ice cubes.
2. Cover with the lid, press 'high', then press 'pulse' and let the ingredients blend until incorporated and smooth.
3. Add ice cubes into the jar, cover with the lid and then pulse until slushy.
4. Divide slush between four bowls and then serve.

Nutrition Value:

- Calories: 112 Cal
- Fat: 0 g
- Carbs: 30 g
- Protein: 1 g
- Fiber: 2 g

Chapter 6: Condiments and Sauces

Pistachio Milk

Preparation time: 10 minutes

Cooking time: 0 minute

Servings: 4

Ingredients:

- 1 cup roasted pistachios
- 1 teaspoon vanilla extract. unsweetened
- 4 cups water

Method:

1. Rinse the pistachios.
2. Plug in and switch on the NutriBullet blender, add pistachios into the jar along with vanilla extract and then pour in water.
3. Cover with the lid, press 'high', then press 'pulse' and let the ingredients blend until incorporated and smooth.
4. Take a large jar, cover its mouth with a cheesecloth and then slowly sift the cashew mixture through the cloth.
5. Remove clothe from the jar, and then cool the milk in the jar into the refrigerator for 4 to 6 hours until chilled.
6. Serve straight away.

Nutrition Value:

- Calories: 175.5 Cal

- Fat: 13.1 g
- Carbs: 8.8 g
- Protein: 5.7 g
- Fiber: 3.2 g

Tomato Marinara Sauce

Preparation time: 5 minutes

Cooking time: 28 minutes

Servings: 4

Ingredients:

- 2 cups vegetable broth
- 1/3 cup sundried tomatoes, packed in oil
- 1 teaspoon sea salt
- 4 cloves of garlic, peeled, roasted, cooled
- 1 tablespoon sugar
- ½ of medium white onion, peeled, roasted, cooled
- 2 tablespoons tomato paste, unsalted
- 1/4 cup basil
- 1 teaspoon Italian seasoning
- 1 teaspoon dried oregano
- 1/4 teaspoon ground black pepper

Method:

1. Plug in and switch on the NutriBullet blender and then add all the ingredients in the order into the jar.
2. Cover with the lid, press 'high', then press 'pulse' and let the ingredients blend until incorporated and smooth.
3. Take a medium pot, place it over medium heat, pour in blended sauce, bring it a simmer and then continue simmering for 25 minutes until reach to desired consistency.

4. When done, remove pot from heat and ladle sauce over cooked pasta.

5. Serve straight away.

Nutrition Value:

- Calories: 46.4 Cal
- Fat: 0.2 g
- Carbs: 10.7 g
- Protein: 1.4 g
- Fiber: 1.3 g

Red Salsa

Preparation time: 8 minutes

Cooking time: 0 minute

Servings: 6

Ingredients:

- ½ of medium white onion, peeled, cut into two quarters
- 2 Anaheim pepper, quartered
- 3 cloves of garlic, peeled
- ½ cup cilantro leaves
- 1 teaspoon sea salt
- 1/4 cup dried Chile de Arbol, toasted
- 1 teaspoon sugar
- 2 tablespoons lime juice
- 2 cups diced tomatoes

Method:

1. Plug in and switch on the NutriBullet blender and then add all the ingredients in the order into the jar except for tomatoes.
2. Cover with the lid, press 'high', then press 'pulse' and let the ingredients blend until incorporated and smooth.
3. Add tomatoes, pulse for 3 to 4 minutes until tomatoes break down and mixture has reached to salsa consistency.
4. Tip the salsa into a medium bowl and then serve it with tortilla chips.

Nutrition Value:

- Calories: 39.2 Cal
- Fat: 0.2 g
- Carbs: 6 g
- Protein: 1 g
- Fiber: 2 g

Guacamole

Preparation time: 5 minutes

Cooking time: 0 minute

Servings: 6

Ingredients:

- ½ of medium red onion, peeled, cut into quarters
- 2 jalapeno peppers, deseeded, quartered
- 3 cloves of garlic, peeled
- ½ cup cilantro leaves
- 1 teaspoon sea salt
- 1 teaspoon ground black pepper
- 2 tablespoons lime juice
- 2 avocado, peeled, pitted, flesh cut into quarters

Method:

1. Plug in and switch on the NutriBullet blender and then add all the ingredients in the order into the jar except for avocado.
2. Cover with the lid, press 'high', then press 'pulse' and let the ingredients blend until incorporated and smooth.
3. Add avocado, pulse for 3 to 4 minutes until avocado break down and thick mixture comes together.
4. Tip the guacamole into a medium bowl and then serve it with tortilla chips.

Nutrition Value:

- Calories: 89.4 Cal

- Fat: 7.4 g
- Carbs: 6.5 g
- Protein: 1.3 g
- Fiber: 3.8 g

Cashew Creamer

Preparation time: 5 minutes

Cooking time: 0 minute

Servings: 128

Ingredients:

- 6 cups of water
- 3 cups cashews, soaked in warm water for 1 hour
- 4 Medjool dates, pitted
- 1/8 teaspoon sea salt
- 1 teaspoon vanilla extract, unsweetened

Method:

1. Plug in and switch on the NutriBullet blender and then add all the ingredients in the order into the jar.
2. Cover with the lid, press 'high', then press 'pulse' and let the ingredients blend until incorporated and smooth.
3. Serve creamer with coffee.

Nutrition Value:

- Calories: 19.9 Cal
- Fat: 1.4 g
- Carbs: 1.5 g
- Protein: 0.6 g
- Fiber: 0.2 g

Hummus

Preparation time: 5 minutes

Cooking time: 0 minute

Servings: 32

Ingredients:

- 3 cups canned chickpeas
- 2 cloves of garlic, peeled
- 1/4 cup and 2 teaspoons lemon juice
- 1/4 cup olive oil
- 1/3 cup water
- 1/2 cup tahini
- 1/2 teaspoon sea salt
- 1/4 teaspoon ground cumin

Method:

1. Plug in and switch on the NutriBullet blender and then add all the ingredients in the order into the jar.
2. Cover with the lid, press 'high', and then pulse for 3 to 5 minutes until chickpeas are broken and thick mixture comes together.
3. Tip the hummus into a bowl, sprinkle with red chili powder, drizzle with some more olive oil and then serve.

Nutrition Value:

- Calories: 58.1 Cal
- Fat: 4.1 g

- Carbs: 4.3 g
- Protein: 1.7 g
- Fiber: 1.1 g

Pesto

Preparation time: 5 minutes

Cooking time: 0 minute

Servings: 2

Ingredients:

- 1 1/4 cup olive oil
- 3 cups basil leaves
- 1/2 teaspoon sea salt
- 1 ½ cup dried pine nuts, dried
- 1/2 teaspoon ground black pepper
- 8 cloves of garlic
- 2 cups grated parmesan cheese

Method:

1. Plug in and switch on the NutriBullet blender and then add all the ingredients in the order into the jar.
2. Cover with the lid, press 'high' and then pulse for five time for 3 seconds.
3. Then press 'low' button and continue blending the pesto for 30 seconds until smooth.
4. Tip pesto into a bowl and then serve.

Nutrition Value:

- Calories: 236.7 Cal
- Fat: 23.7 g
- Carbs: 3.2 g
- Protein: 4.4 g
- Fiber: 0.5 g

BBQ Sauce

Preparation time: 5 minutes

Cooking time: 0 minute

Servings: 30

Ingredients:

- 2 tablespoons honey
- 1 cup ketchup
- 2 tablespoons Worcestershire sauce
- 1/3 cup apple cider vinegar

Method:

1. Plug in and switch on the NutriBullet blender and then add all the ingredients in the order into the jar.
2. Cover with the lid, press 'high', then press 'pulse' and let the ingredients blend until incorporated and smooth.
3. Tip BBQ sauce into a bowl or a jar and then use as desired.

Nutrition Value:

- Calories: 13.7 Cal
- Fat: 0 g
- Carbs: 0 g
- Protein: 0.1 g
- Fiber: 0 g

Hollandaise Sauce

Preparation time: 5 minutes

Cooking time: 1 minute

Servings: 6

Ingredients:

- 1/4 teaspoon Dijon mustard
- 1/8 teaspoon Tabasco sauce
- 1 tablespoon lemon juice
- 3 egg yolks
- 1/2 cup butter, unsalted

Method:

1. Plug in and switch on the NutriBullet blender and then add all the ingredients in the order into the jar except for butter.
2. Cover with the lid, press 'high', then press 'pulse' and let the ingredients blend until smooth.
3. Take a medium heatproof bowl, place butter in it and then microwave for 1 minute at high heat setting until it melts and hot.
4. Gradually blend butter into the egg mixture until thick sauce comes together and.
5. Keep sauce warm by placing the jar into a pot containing warm water until ready to serve.

Nutrition Value:

- Calories: 163 Cal
- Fat: 17.5 g

- Carbs: 0.6 g
- Protein: 1.5 g
- Fiber: 0 g

Cranberry and Fig Jam

Preparation time: 5 minutes

Cooking time: 4 minutes

Servings: 20

Ingredients:

- 1 cup orange juice
- 1 cup dry cranberries, sweetened
- 2 tablespoons grated ginger
- 1 cup dried figs, dried
- 1 teaspoon vanilla extract, unsweetened

Method:

1. Take a large heatproof bowl, place all the ingredients in it except for vanilla and then microwave for 4 minutes at high heat setting until ingredients turn soft.
2. Add vanilla, stir until mixed and then transfer the mixture into a jar of NutriBullet blender.
3. Plug in and switch on the blender, cover with the lid, press 'high', then press 'pulse' for four times until all the ingredients have broken.
4. Tip the jam into a bowl and then serve.

Nutrition Value:

- Calories: 50.2 Cal
- Fat: 0.2 g
- Carbs: 13 g
- Protein: 0.4 g
- Fiber: 1.2 g

Conclusion

In today's busy lifestyle where we are racing against time, we hardly take out time to buy these healthy ingredients, and then managing time to cook them is another ball game. Therefore, people aren't just getting enough veggies and fruits in their diet, and thus, their unhealthy diet ends them up suffering harmful ailments. But there is a way to get more out of vegetables and fruits into your diet and requires far less time compared to cooking. The secret is sipping your food on the go by using blending. And, Nutribullet Blender ZNBF30400Z Machine is an inexpensive and convenient appliance to start your journey in the wonderful world of blending. With Nutribullet Blender, you know what you are feeding your body, and you can variety of options to tickle your taste buds and satisfy your stomach, without any eating.

Take advantage of the benefits of Nutribullet Blender and make your collection of delicious blending recipes.

Happy blending!

CPSIA information can be obtained
at www.ICGtesting.com
Printed in the USA
LVHW100345251120
672555LV00014B/286